A Child's First Library of Learning

Life in the Water

TIME-LIFE BOOKS • ALEXANDRIA, VIRGINIA

Contents

❓ Why Do Fish Have Scales?

ANSWER Fish have soft bodies. They need hard scales to protect their bodies. Most fish have scales that look a little like shingles on a roof. The scales bend and slide over one another so that the fish is able to move.

CRAZY-LOOKING FISH!

▲ **Pinecone fish.** It has large, thick scales. It can't swim very fast, perhaps because its scales are so heavy.

■ Look at these scales

▲ **Porcupine fish.** It has scales like needles. To protect itself it makes the needles stand up.

▲ **Coffin fish.** It has hard scales all over its body. It can move only its fins and its mouth.

▲ **Shark.** It has very small pointed scales. If you touch them they feel rough.

■ Scales tell the age

Rings in the scale tell us a fish's age.

▲ **Sea bream scale**

❓ Are There Any Fish That Don't Have Scales?

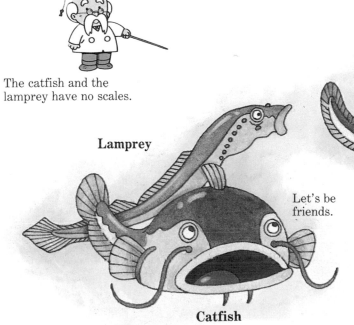

The catfish and the lamprey have no scales.

Lamprey

Let's be friends.

Catfish

Eel

We've got scales!

Loach

The loach and the eel have tiny scales.

● To the Parent

Scales and a mucous membrane protect the surface of a fish's body. Almost all types of fish, including sharks and eels, have scales, although a shark's tiny scales are visible only under a microscope, and an eel's scales are buried under its skin. Generally, the fish that are fast swimmers have light, thin scales that form only on areas where they are necessary.

❓ Why Do Fish Die If They're Out of Water?

ANSWER Fish need oxygen to live. They get it as water passes over their gills. A fish's gills work only when it is in water. That's why most fish will die if they are left out of water too long.

People, along with animals like dogs and birds, use their lungs to take oxygen out of the air.

MINI-DATA

A fish takes in water through its mouth, then lets it flow out over the gills. The fish breathes this way.

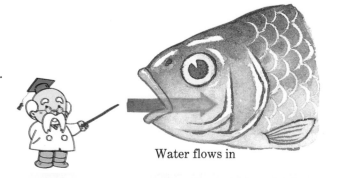

Water flows in

Water flows out

Some Fish Can Live Even When They're Not in Water

▲ **Climbing perch.** It can breathe air, so it can stay on dry land for long periods of time.

▲ **Mudskipper.** It moves from one mudpuddle to the next. When it's out of the water, the mudskipper breathes by swallowing air.

▲ **Lungfish.** In the dry season, when there isn't enough water, it digs a hole. Inside the hole it breathes air through its lungs.

▲ **Snakehead.** This fish, which lives in Africa and Asia, has special chambers near its gills for breathing. It can survive for long periods out of water and hibernates in mud during the summer.

● **To the Parent**

Shock is the major cause of a fish's death when it is taken out of the water. But even if a fish can be removed from the water without its going into shock, it will still die. People, birds and other land animals use their lungs to take oxygen out of the air, but fish must get oxygen from the water with their gills. This oxygen is carried throughout the fish's body by the bloodstream, which takes carbon dioxide back to the gills to be exchanged for more oxygen. Some fish, like the lungfish, depend on both gills and lungs to get oxygen.

7

⍰ Did You Know That Fish Have Ears?

(ANSWER) When a fish hears something like a voice or footsteps, it will swim to the bottom to be safe. Fish can hear well because they have good ears, one on each side of their head. But you can't see them from the outside the way you can see a person's ears.

Looking down from above

Ear

Ear

Do Fish Have Noses Too?

Yes, they do have. Some fish find food by smelling for it. Usually fish have two nostrils on each side of their head. Water comes in the front nostril, then goes out the back one. In this way the fish can smell what's in the water.

Smells so good!!

Carp's nose

Water flow

This is the nose. The fish uses it to pick up the smells of many things in the water.

▲ A school of red carp

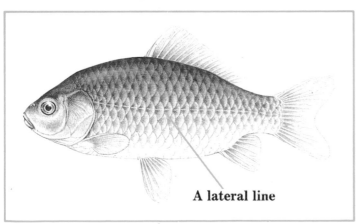

A lateral line

A fish can pick up even very low sounds through a special line on each side of its body called a lateral line.

❓ Do Fish Go to Sleep?

ANSWER Yes, fish sleep too. Have you ever seen a goldfish lying quietly at the bottom of its bowl? It probably was asleep even though its eyes were open. Because fish have no eyelids, they can't close their eyes. Goldfish sleep at night. But some fish, like the loach, sleep in the daytime and move around during the night.

Loach sleep in the daytime.

Minnows and goldfish sleep at night.

10

Here Are Some Places Where Fish Sleep

▲ **Rabbit fish.** At night it turns on its side and sleeps in a crack in the rocks.

▲ **Forked crucian carp.** It sleeps inside beds of coral at night.

▲ **Conger eel.** It sleeps in the sand during the day with only its head sticking out. At night it moves around.

11

What Are Some Odd Ways That Fish Care for Their Young?

(ANSWER) Most fish lay eggs and don't bother any more about them. When they hatch, young fish get their own food. But some, such as the mouthbreeder, do look after their young.

The topminnow just lays eggs, then doesn't do anything else.

If there's danger nearby, the tilapia protects its young by holding them in its mouth.

Here's What Some Fish Do

▲ This male fish looks after the eggs until they hatch.

▲ When the male bumps the eggs, the young jump out.

▲ Adult discus fish feed their young with a milky fluid from their bodies.

● To the Parent

The tilapia is known as a mouthbreeder. Varying from 4 to 12 inches (10-30 cm) long, it is a native of eastern and southern Africa. The tilapia can live in dirty or brackish water and in warm water, but it is vulnerable to the cold and will die if the water temperature should drop too low. Immediately after she lays her eggs, the female gathers them into her mouth and goes to stay in water where there are many water plants. As soon as the eggs hatch, she stands guard until the young have grown big enough to take care of themselves.

? Why Do Minnows Swim Around Together?

ANSWER A minnow is very small. It has no weapons to protect itself from attacks by enemies. If minnows stay together, some of them will be able to get away even if they are attacked. That's why they swim around together.

● **To the Parent**

In the animal world the weak are eaten by the stronger, and the strong are eaten in turn by even stronger creatures. Every species of animal has some means of self-defense and survival. Smaller and weaker animals like minnows have no weapons with which they can protect themselves against enemies, but they can survive by swimming together in schools. If the minnows are attacked some of them may be eaten, but the majority will scatter in all directions and manage to escape their attacker.

There Are Other Fish That Stay Together for Safety

▲ **Sardines.** They swim in very large schools.

◄ **Marine catfish.** During the day they swim in schools and stay safe. But at night they separate and go off to hunt for food. Their fins are poisonous.

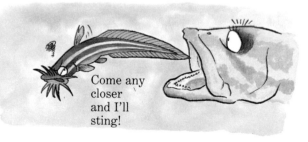

Come any closer and I'll sting!

$\boxed{\text{MINI-DATA}}$

If some minnows are put into a bowl holding still water they swim in all directions. But if the water is stirred so that it flows around the bowl, the minnows will all swim in the same direction against the current caused by stirring.

Stir it.

They all swim the same way.

Why Do We Put Water Plants In a Goldfish Bowl?

ANSWER Because the plants give off oxygen. Goldfish need oxygen to live. If there's not enough of it in the water, the goldfish will die. Water plants give fish the oxygen they need.

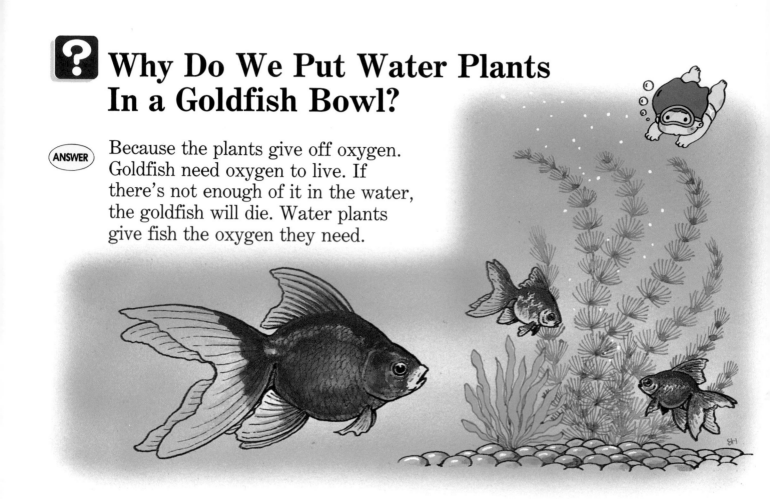

ANSWER Goldfish also lay their eggs among plants, so be sure there are lots of plants in your bowl in spring and summer. That is when the goldfish lay their eggs.

ANSWER Plants also give the weaker fish a place to hide. There are different kinds and sizes of goldfish. Smaller and weaker fish can swim away and hide among the water plants if the bigger fish bully them.

What Can We Do If We Don't Have Water Plants?

You should use a special pump called an aerator. It's a machine that adds oxygen to the water in the goldfish bowl. You could also put some stones in the bowl. With those, the smaller fish will have a place to hide from the larger fish.

● **To the Parent**

The reasons for putting water plants into your fishbowl are valid not only for goldfish but for other species of fish as well. For minnows, however, water plants are not necessary to encourage the laying of eggs. When it is dark, water plants absorb oxygen, so they can be counterproductive. If you use water plants, be sure they get enough light. The plants help keep the water clean by absorbing through their roots some of the animal waste matter. This mutual dependency is called symbiosis, and through it fish and plant help each other live.

? Did You Know That Goldfish Are Very Dark When They Hatch?

ANSWER When goldfish hatch from their eggs they're a dark color, almost black. As they grow bigger most of them turn an orange color. Some, though, turn white instead of orange as they grow bigger.

A goldfish that has just hatched.

Slowly it turns orange.

Young goldfish

● **To the Parent**

Goldfish were first bred in ancient China as decorative fish. They were produced through selective breeding of a particular variety of carp that displayed orange coloring. Today some commercially bred goldfish still owe their origin directly to that fish, while some others are the result of cross-breeding. The beautiful *nishiki* carp was bred in Japan.

Now it's a
splendid goldfish.

MINI-DATA

A fish called a crucian carp
is the ancestor of the goldfish.
The goldfish came from a relative of
the crucian that had an orange color.

Crucian carp ▶

The ancestor of
the goldfish.

❓ Why Does This Fish Puff Up?

ANSWER The globefish puffs itself up so it will look bigger and scare away its enemies.

▲ It takes in water and makes its body swell up.

◀ A globefish usually looks like this.

■ How a globefish swells

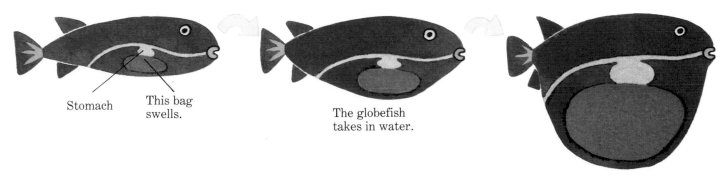

Stomach   This bag swells.

The globefish takes in water.

 ## Do Other Animals Make Themselves Look Bigger?

Lots of animals protect themselves this way. They make their bodies look bigger in various ways so they can scare away their enemies.

▲ A mantis protects itself by raising its legs and spreading its wings.

▲ When a cat gets ready to fight, it fluffs up its body to scare an enemy.

▲ When an enemy approaches, a young owl spreads its feathers to look bigger.

● To the Parent

The globefish takes in water and holds it in a passage that leads to its stomach. Several kinds of globefish use this ability, not only as a reaction to danger. They can swell up suddenly if they wish to stir up the sand on the bottom so that they can locate food more easily. If a globefish is removed from the water it takes in air, but it still swells.

Why Do Sharks Attack People?

ANSWER Sharks eat fish, squid and other things in the sea. Most sharks are very peaceful and never bother people. But some, like the great white shark and the bonito shark, will attack people. They have very sharp teeth and usually eat big fish. To a shark, a person is like a big fish—just something else for it to eat.

Great white shark
This man-eating shark has sharp teeth
that point inward. When the jaws close
on something, the teeth don't let go
until they have bitten off a piece.

The Shark's Secrets

A shark can hear sounds from far away.

A shark can also smell blood from far away. Its nose is very good at picking up the smell of blood. When a shark smells blood it will rush toward it.

A shark has to keep moving. It can't breathe unless it stays on the move. If a shark gets trapped between two rocks it will die because it can't breathe.

● To the Parent

There are about 250 species of shark. The largest is the whale shark, which measures 60 feet (18 m) in length. The smallest, the dwarf shark, is only six inches (15 cm) long. All sharks are carnivorous, but only a few species will attack people. Though certain sharks are rightly famous for their ferocity, your child will be relieved to know that shark attacks are quite rare.

■ Dangerous sharks

Bonito shark

Hammerhead shark

Great white shark

❓ Do Flying Fish Really Fly?

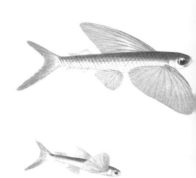

ANSWER Flying fish really do fly through the air.
If an enemy chases them they swim very fast
and then leap out of the water. By spreading
out their very large fins they can soar like
an airplane. As they come shooting out of the
water they shake their tail to make themselves
go even faster. After they're in the air they
can control their direction by using their fins.

Look! A big fish!

Let's get away!

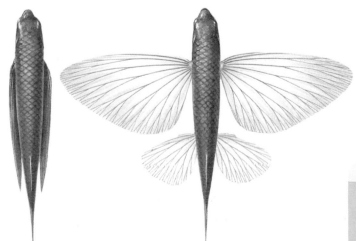

Fins folded　　　　**Fins spread**

They fly like hang gliders, don't they?

● **To the Parent**

The flying fish and its relatives live in warm seas. They are able to glide through the air with the help of their well-developed pectoral and pelvic fins, or in some species with pectoral fins alone. Some of the larger flying fish can soar more than 330 yards (300 m) with the wind behind them.

❓ Why Do Flounders Have Both Eyes On the Same Side?

(ANSWER) Flatfish like the flounder spend their lives lying close to the bottom of the sea. Because they lie on one side all the time, both their eyes are on the other side, or the top, of their body.

▲ **The flounder's face.** Both eyes are on the left side of its body.

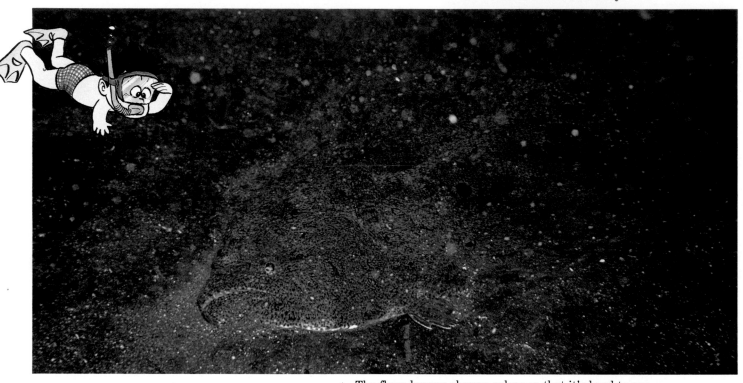

▲ The flounder can change colors so that it's hard to see.

Life on the Seabed

It's easy to hide.

And it's easy to find food.

■ A flounder's food

Shrimp

Shellfish

Fish

Starfish

Crab

26

When the Fish Is Young It Has Eyes on Both Sides

When the flounder is young it has one eye on each side of its head and swims in an upright position the same way most other fish do. But as it grows older and begins to live on the bottom of the sea the lower eye starts to move and continues until it is on top of the fish's head. The same thing occurs in many other species of flatfish.

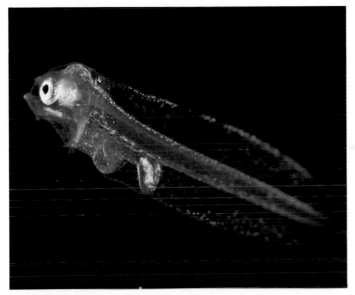

▲ A young flounder, just out of the egg.

▲ The eyes are still on both sides.

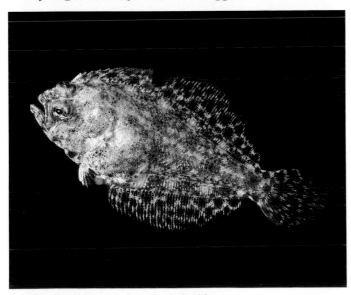

▲ The eye has moved to the left side.

▲ The eye on the right side is moving.

● **To the Parent**

The eyes of most plaice are on the right side of the body, but flounders' eyes are usually on the left. When these fish have grown to about an inch (2.5 cm) they begin to live on the seabed, where they lie on their side. The underside then fades to white, and the bottom eye shifts around to the top.

![?] What Are These Creatures Doing?

■ A crayfish sheds its old shell

As a crayfish grows, it has to get out of its old shell. This is called molting.

■ Goldfish that need air

When the water doesn't have enough oxygen in it, the fish have trouble breathing. Before this happens, the water should be changed. Or more oxygen should be added to it.

■ These fish are on guard

The sea urchins' spines protect the small fish from big fish who would like to eat them.

■ A mouthbreeder protects its young by keeping them in its mouth

For a while after they've hatched, the baby fish hide inside their mother's mouth. That's why this kind of fish is called a mouthbreeder.

■ Baby mud snails are being born

When mud snails are born, they're covered with a thin membrane. It's like a soft layer of tissue over the baby snail.

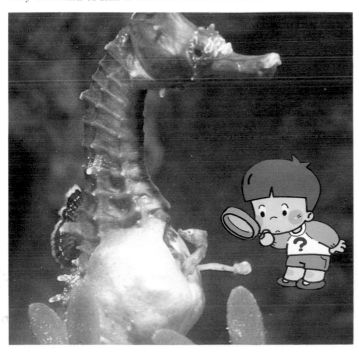

■ A male seahorse is giving birth to its young

The female seahorse puts her eggs into a pouch on the male's stomach. The eggs hatch in the pouch after eight or ten days. When the young come out into the water, they look just like adult seahorses except that they're smaller.

■ This wrasse is eating tiny animals called parasites from a fish's gills

● **To the Parent**

Animals whose bodies are protected by a hard shell cannot grow larger than the shell. From time to time they molt, or shed their shell, so that they can continue growing. When there is not enough oxygen in the water, goldfish will go to the surface and gulp air. One ayu species protects itself by hiding among the poison spines of a particular sea urchin.

? Why Is an Octopus's Head So Big?

ANSWER The octopus looks as though it has a big head. But the part that seems to be its head is really its body. Inside it are the stomach, heart and other organs. The octopus has a tiny head inside its body. You can see where the head is in the picture below.

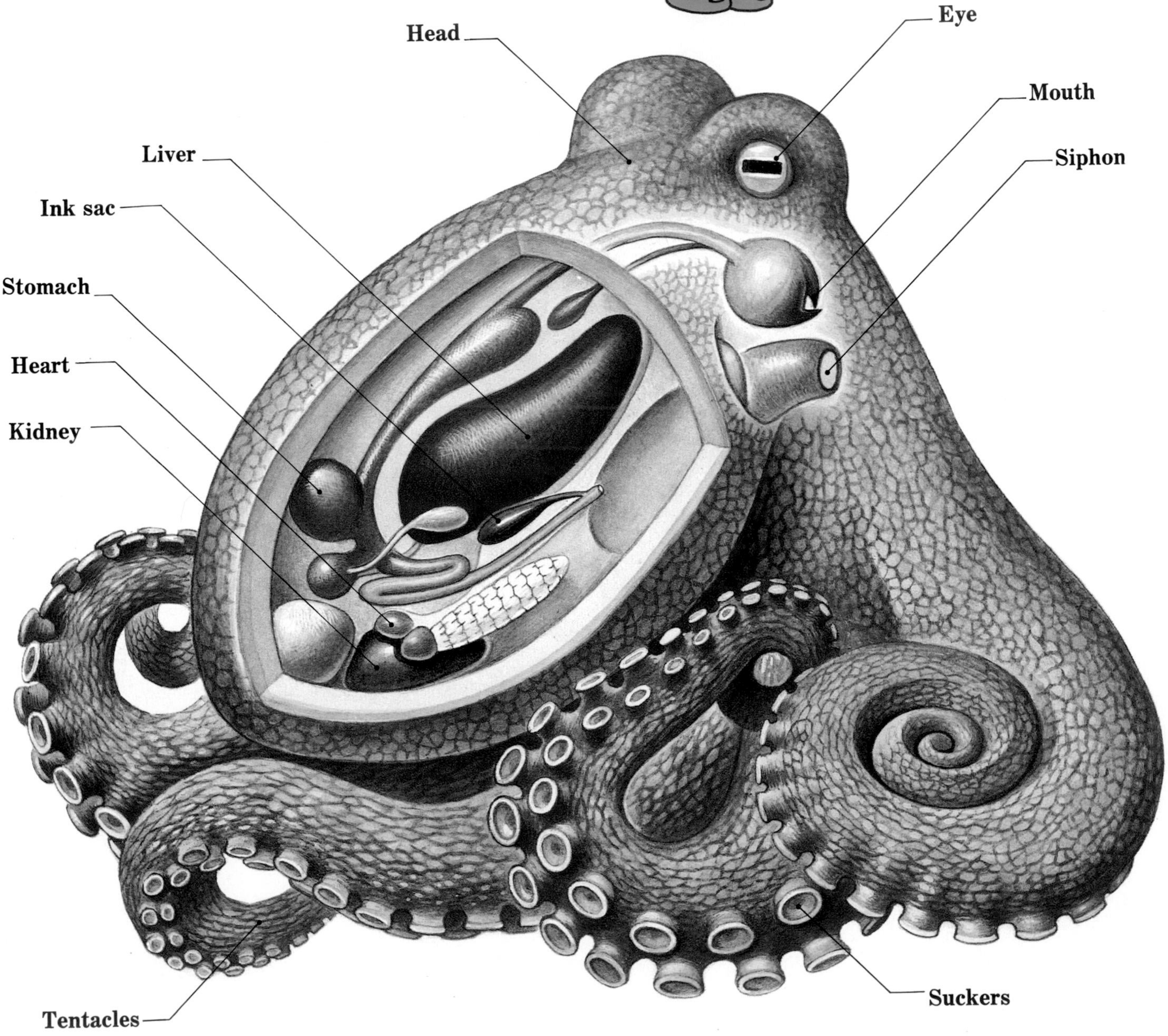

Head

Eye

Mouth

Liver

Siphon

Ink sac

Stomach

Heart

Kidney

Tentacles

Suckers

How an Octopus Lives

It lies and waits to catch something to eat.

It reaches out and catches food.

It shoots poison into a shellfish to make it open.

It swims by shooting out water.

It holds onto things with suckers on its tentacles.

■ Other sea animals give off ink

All of them use ink to protect themselves.

▲ **Squid.** It gives off black ink.

▲ **Sea hare.** Its ink is purple.

▲ **Octopus.** It squirts out ink and escapes.

● To the Parent

What appears to be the head of an octopus is actually its body with the vital organs inside. The head is between the body and the tentacles. The octopus and the squid are called cephalopods because their tentacles, or legs, are connected to their head. The ink of an octopus works like a protective smoke screen. The squid's ink draws attention away from the squid, while that of a sea hare actually repels its enemies.

? Why Do Some Fish Have Whiskers?

ANSWER Some fish like the carp and loach have whiskers to help them find food. By touching something with their whiskers they know whether they can eat it. They can even tell if the food tastes good. Several kinds of catfish have whiskers too. They swim along near the bottom looking for food.

Carp. It has four whiskers.

Loach. It has ten whiskers.

Mullet. It has only two whiskers. It swims along the bottom looking for food. When it isn't using its whiskers it folds them away.

Catfish. This gold one has eight whiskers.

Catfish. It also has eight whiskers.

Catfish. This big one has only four whiskers.

● **To the Parent**

The whiskers of fish are sensory organs used to touch and taste. Most fish that have whiskers swim along the bottom as they search for food. If you observe loaches in an aquarium you will see that they use their whiskers as they scavenge along the bottom for food. If they are in the same water as goldfish, they are very useful in keeping the aquarium clean.

Why Does a Hermit Crab Change Homes?

ANSWER The hermit crab doesn't live in its own shell. It lives in one it finds on the beach. When the crab gets too large for that shell it must change homes.

So crowded!
Can't stay here.

▲ This looks just about right.

▲ Here we go! I just back into it, and I've finished moving.

34

■ Measuring for size

Before it moves into a new shell, the hermit crab checks the size. It uses its claws to measure the shell and be sure that the size is right.

Looks a bit large.

❓ But Why Does a Hermit Crab Need a Shell?

The hermit crab is a relative of the other crabs and of shrimps, too. As you know, crabs and shrimps have hard shells to protect their body. But a hermit crab has a soft body without a hard shell. So it moves into a spiral shell for protection.

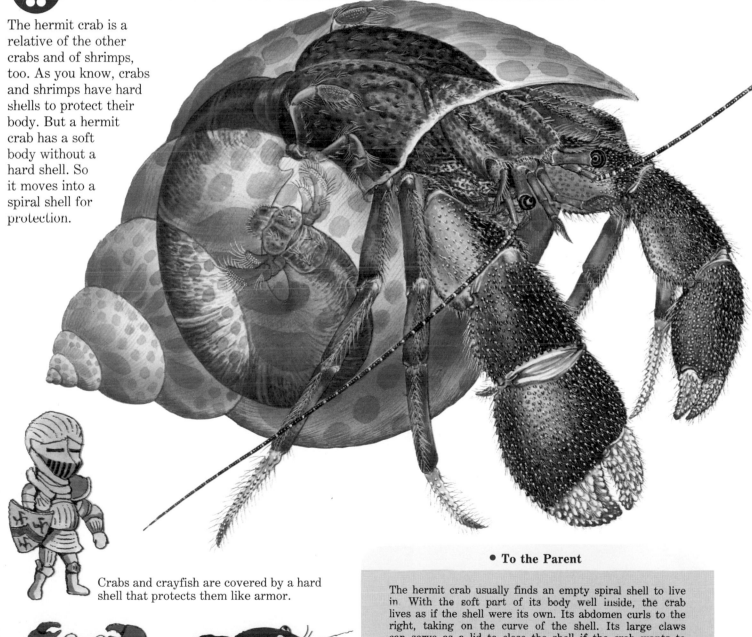

Crabs and crayfish are covered by a hard shell that protects them like armor.

• **To the Parent**

The hermit crab usually finds an empty spiral shell to live in. With the soft part of its body well inside, the crab lives as if the shell were its own. Its abdomen curls to the right, taking on the curve of the shell. Its large claws can serve as a lid to close the shell if the crab wants to hide inside. When a hermit crab looks for a larger shell, it investigates carefully. The kind of shell is not important, but the size is. If you keep a hermit crab, provide it with a variety of shells. You may be able to watch it change houses.

Why Do Crabs Walk Sideways?

(ANSWER) It's easy for people to move their legs forward or backward. That's because of the way they're attached to the body. People's knees bend toward the front, and that also makes it easy to walk forward. But a crab's legs are attached to the sides of its body. And its joints, unlike our knees, bend so that the crab can walk sideways. That's why crabs walk the way they do. Can you do it?

■ How a crab walks sideways

But Do All Crabs Walk Sideways?

Some crabs can walk forward. Those crabs have shells that are longer than they are wide. Crabs that walk sideways have shells that are wider than they are long.

Walks sideways   Walks forward

▲ **Frog crab.** It walks forward the way you do.

▲ **A Taiwan crab.** It is a good swimmer.

Some other animals go sideways too. A rattlesnake called the sidewinder slithers sideways as it loops across the desert.

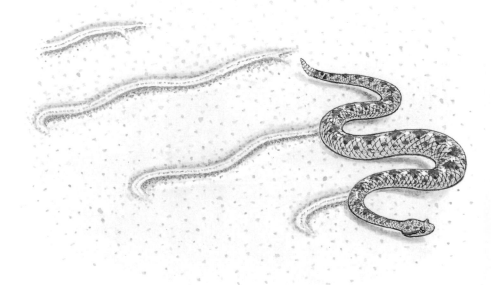

? Why Do Crabs Foam at the Mouth?

(ANSWER) If you see a crab foaming at the mouth, it means the crab is having trouble breathing. Like all animals, crabs need oxygen to live. They take oxygen from the water, through their gills, as fish do. Even when crabs are on land they can use the water stored inside their gills. But they can do this for only a little while. When their gills start to dry out, it becomes hard for crabs to breathe. They begin to move their mouth and gills, trying to take in water. But only air comes in, and the water still in the gills turns to foam.

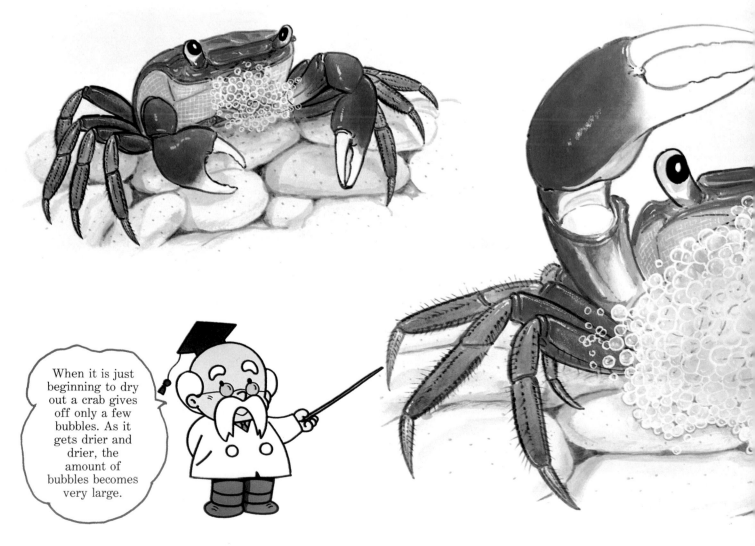

When it is just beginning to dry out a crab gives off only a few bubbles. As it gets drier and drier, the amount of bubbles becomes very large.

▲ A crab's gills are like a sponge.

● **To the Parent**

Crabs, like fish, get oxygen through their gills. A crab's gills are spongy, and it can easily take in water. For that reason, a crab can live for quite some time on land, using the water held inside its gills. Eventually, however, the gills dry out or the store of oxygen is exhausted, and the crab begins to be uncomfortable. It contorts its mouth and gills trying to get water, but only air enters. The air is mixed with whatever water is still in the gills, and foam is produced. The staler the crab's water, the more foam there is.

How Does a Crayfish Use Its Claws?

It waits for fish to come out of their hiding places.

ANSWER A crayfish uses its large claws to catch food like tadpoles and fish. If the fish is large, the crayfish cuts it up with the smaller claws on its other legs. That way it's easier to eat. If the crayfish catches a tiny fish or something else small, it eats it whole, without cutting it up.

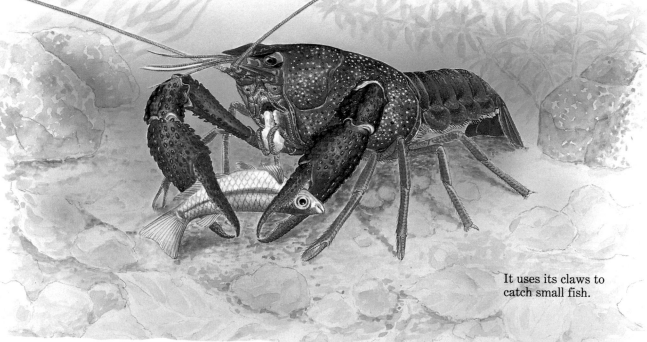

It uses its claws to catch small fish.

The crayfish snaps rice plants off at the ground with its claws. For that reason farmers don't like to have it in their paddy fields.

Its smaller claws cut up food.

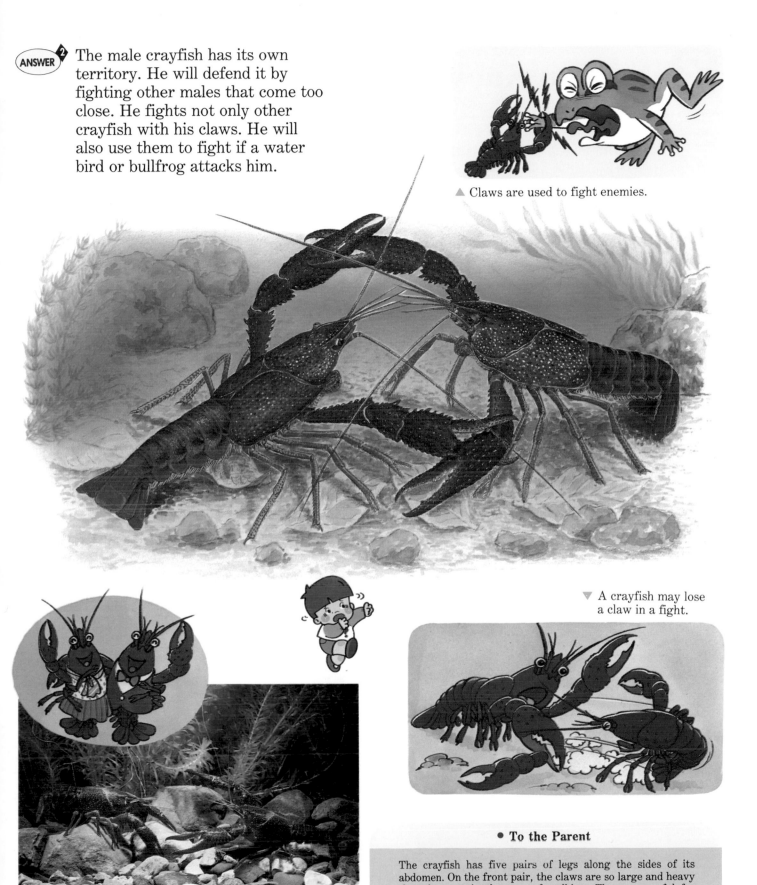

ANSWER ❷ The male crayfish has its own territory. He will defend it by fighting other males that come too close. He fights not only other crayfish with his claws. He will also use them to fight if a water bird or bullfrog attacks him.

▲ Claws are used to fight enemies.

▼ A crayfish may lose a claw in a fight.

▲ A male and female crayfish get acquainted. The male's claws are bigger than the female's.

● **To the Parent**

The crayfish has five pairs of legs along the sides of its abdomen. On the front pair, the claws are so large and heavy that they get in the way of walking. They are useful for catching food, however, and for fighting. Facing an enemy, the crayfish may wave its claws about to display strength, using them in somewhat the same way a person uses his hands.

❓ Did You Know That a Shrimp Can Swim?

(ANSWER) When something scares a shrimp it swims away backwards. It does this by kicking water out in front with its tail. To swim forward, the shrimp uses its legs. Prawns and shrimp are good at swimming forward. But spiny lobsters and fan shrimp aren't so good at this kind of swimming.

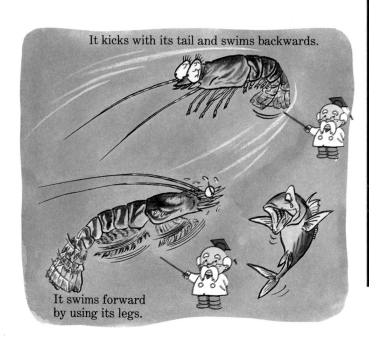

It kicks with its tail and swims backwards.

It swims forward by using its legs.

▲ Some shrimp species swim all the time. They swim in deep water during the day but in shallow water at night.

Some Strong Swimmers

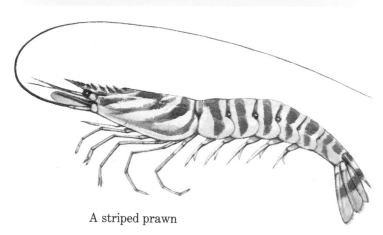

A striped prawn

These two little shrimp are good swimmers.

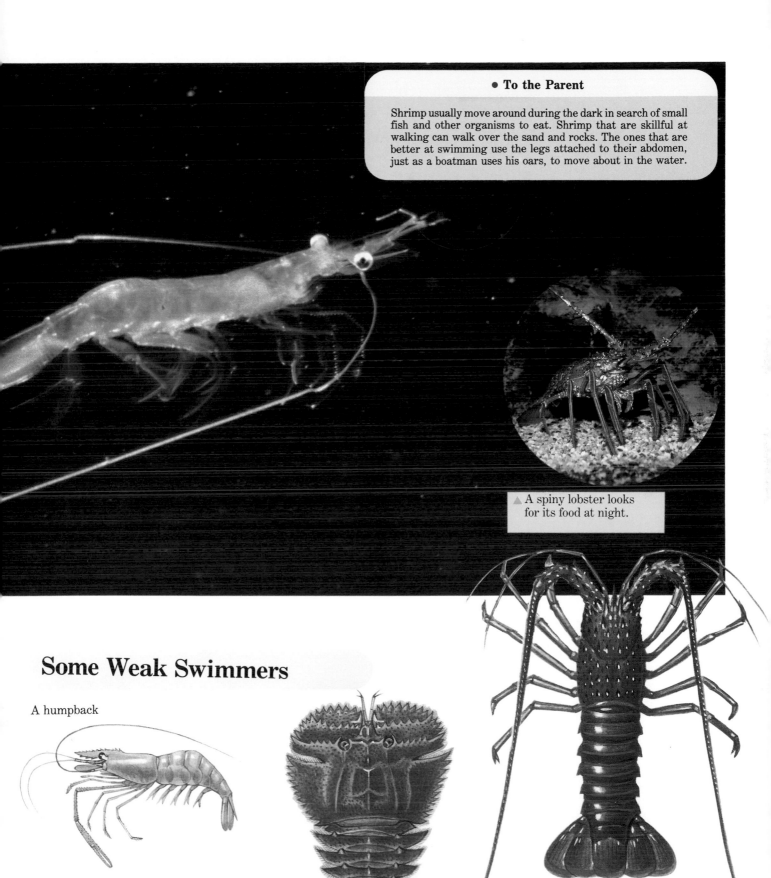

● **To the Parent**

Shrimp usually move around during the dark in search of small fish and other organisms to eat. Shrimp that are skillful at walking can walk over the sand and rocks. The ones that are better at swimming use the legs attached to their abdomen, just as a boatman uses his oars, to move about in the water.

▲ A spiny lobster looks for its food at night.

Some Weak Swimmers

A humpback

Fan shrimp

A big spiny lobster

Can a Shell Grow Larger?

ANSWER Yes, it can. As each shellfish grows larger, its shell must grow larger too. That shell is the animal's home, and it could not live without it. So nature has seen to it that the shell grows. As the shell gets larger, lines appear on it. By studying and counting the rings you can tell the shell's age.

■ **Bivalves**

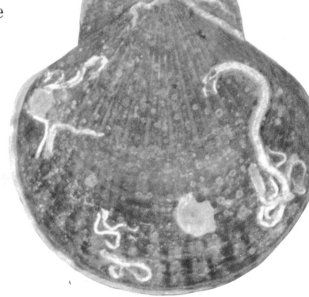

■ **Spirals**

The shell grows larger only in a certain direction.

Bivalve   **Spiral**

As a turban shell gets bigger, it has more horns.

Scallop

Turban shell

▲ **A young bivalve**

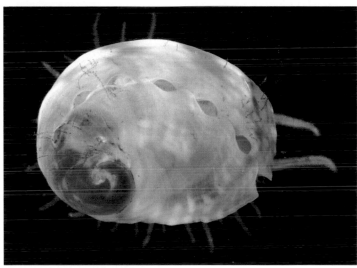

▲ **A young spiral shell**

Just like me.

As a shell grows it leaves a pattern of rings the same way a tree does.

● **To the Parent**

Shells are more than 90% calcium carbonate, which comes from the edges of the membrane around the shellfish's body. As a general rule, shellfish grow more quickly when the water is warm than they do when it is cold. Since the shellfish grows at different seasonal rates, so does the shell. That is why it displays a pattern of lines like a tree's annual rings.

❓ How Do Shellfish Move?

(ANSWER) Shellfish have a kind of foot. The spiral shell's foot is broad and gives off slime as it moves along. The short-necked clam, the true clam and some other shellfish have a foot shaped like an axe. They use their foot to dig into the sand or mud.

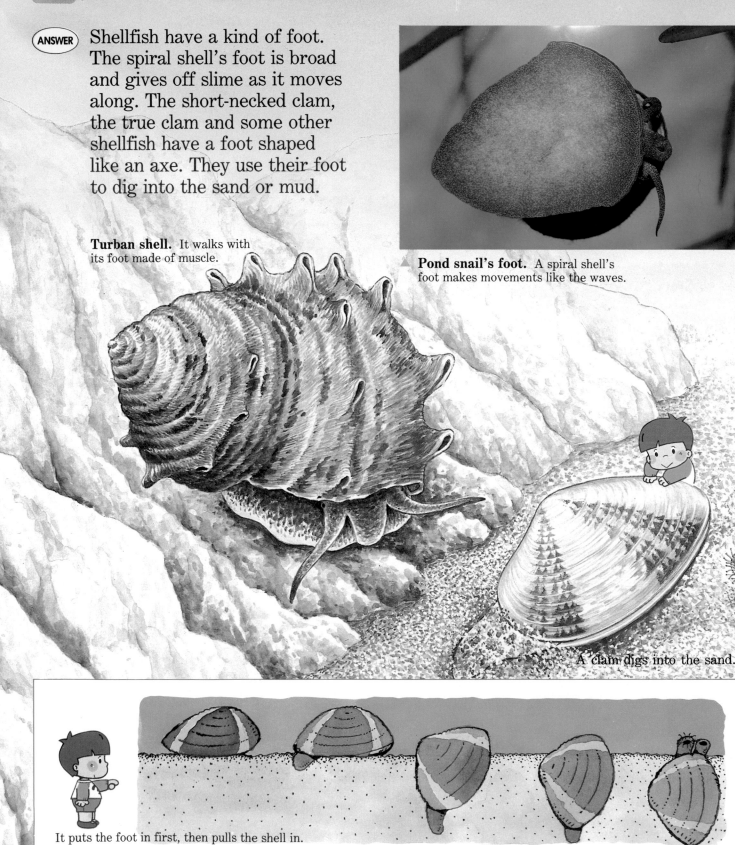

Turban shell. It walks with its foot made of muscle.

Pond snail's foot. A spiral shell's foot makes movements like the waves.

A clam digs into the sand.

It puts the foot in first, then pulls the shell in.

Some shellfish can swim, and some can even jump.

Scallop. It moves by shooting out water.

Periwinkle. It kicks with its foot, then jumps to get away from enemies.

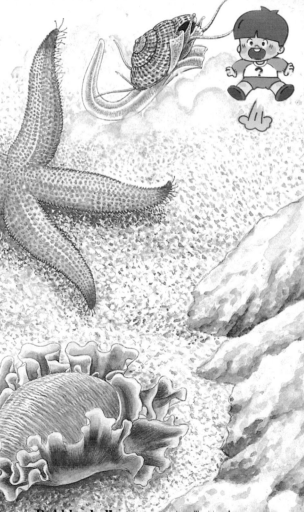

Bubble shell. It moves by fluttering its foot, which is like a big ribbon.

▲ This shell makes a hole in a rock and lives there the rest of its life. On the right you see the broken rock.

▲ Another shell fastens itself to a rock and stays there the rest of its life too.

▲ This strange one makes a raft out of foam. Then it floats along, hanging from the raft.

● **To the Parent**

Bivalves and spiral shells have a muscular organ called a foot or leg. They use it to crawl and to burrow into the sand. If a starfish or other enemy attacks, a bivalve escapes by kicking out with its leg or by closing its shell, shooting out a stream of water and swimming away. Along rocky shores where waves are rough, some shellfish attach themselves to rocks or ledges and remain there for the rest of their lives.

⁇ Did You Know That Scallops Have Eyes?

(ANSWER) Scallops usually live in sand or fine gravel. If you look inside when a scallop's shell opens you can see some round blue things. Those are the scallop's tiny eyes. These eyes can't see the shapes of things, but with them the shellfish can tell whether it's light or dark.

Let's Look Closely at Some Shellfish Eyes

▲ **Scallop.** Here you can see its rows of eyes.

▲ **Mud snail.** It has eyes at the base of its feelers.

 ## Do Any Shellfish Have Ears or a Nose?

Spiral shells have feelers on their head, right in front of the eyes. The feelers are like ears and a nose. They can pick up movements and smells. But bivalves don't have ears or a nose. They don't even have feelers.

Spiral shells use their feelers to pick up smells.

Bivalves take in water through one tube and let it out through another. That's how they get food out of the water.

● **To the Parent**

Only spiral mollusks like the mud snail or the turban shell have eyes or antennae on their head to detect vibrations and smells. The short-necked clam and a considerable number of bivalves related to it are among the many different species of shellfish that have no eyes or antennae. On the outer membrane of some bivalves like the fan shell, however, are short antennae and eyespots that can tell light from dark.

❓ Why Are There Holes In an Abalone's Shell?

(ANSWER) The holes in an abalone's shell let water flow in and out. That's important because an abalone has to take oxygen out of the water with its gills inside the shell. The abalone fastens itself to a rock and doesn't move around. So the holes let it get rid of its wastes, which flow out with the water. And when the abalone lays eggs they come out through the holes in the shell.

An abalone fastens itself tightly to a rock.

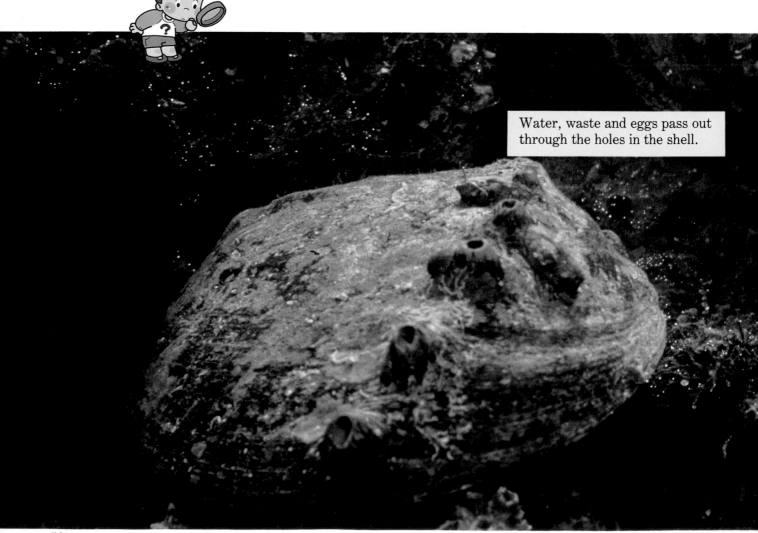

Water, waste and eggs pass out through the holes in the shell.

How Does an Abalone Eat?

An abalone crawls along rocks and eats seaweed that grows on them. Its mouth is in front, on the underside of its body.

Feelers

Its feelers tell the abalone what's around.

When it finds seaweed, it eats.

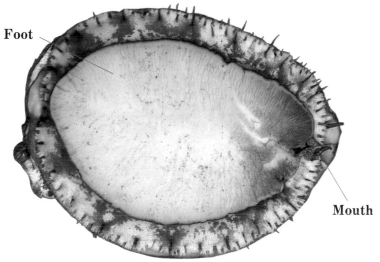

Foot

Mouth

▲ **Abalone.** Seen from underneath.

 MINI-DATA

Look carefully. Can you see the holes on each of the shells?

Abalone

Ear shell

▲ **Abalone crawling over a rock**

● **To the Parent**

The abalone was once thought to be half of a broken bivalve, but actually it is a spiral shellfish. Holes in the abalone's shell allow water to pass in and out, permit the elimination of wastes and are openings through which sperm and eggs are discharged into the water. The abalone's diet consists largely of seaweed, but it also eats leaves that fall into the water.

? How Do Barnacles Eat When They're Fastened to Rocks?

ANSWER Many kinds of sea animals fasten themselves to rocks along the shore. When the tide is out, they keep their mouth tightly closed. When the tide comes in it covers the rocks with water. That's when they open their mouth and start eating.

▲ When waves beat against it this barnacle opens its mouth and eats small water animals.

▲ When it is covered by the sea this one uses its legs to catch small animals living in the water.

Many different sea animals live on rocks.

▲ When the tide is in this wormlike creature extends its hairlike tentacles and catches tiny marine organisms.

▲ When the tide is in this pine-needle shell puts out its legs and moves around eating things like seaweed.

● **To the Parent**

The ocean's tides ebb and flow twice a day. Places on rocky shores that are underwater at high tide are exposed when the tide goes out, and tidal pools are formed. Many kinds of sea animals live in these tidal pools. Several kinds of barnacles and a number of other animals can live on the exposed rocks, entirely out of water, for the short time until the next tide.

？ Did You Know That Sea Urchins Can Walk?

(ANSWER) Among a sea urchin's spines are many legs called tube feet. They're thin tubes that can become longer or shorter, and they can fasten themselves to things with suckers. A sea urchin uses its spines and its tube feet to move around. First it sticks out its feet and fastens them to a rock. Then it makes its feet shorter, and that pulls its body along.

▲ **Sea urchin.** It sticks out its tube feet and walks up the glass side of its aquarium.

Fastening its feet to a rock

Stretching out its feet

 ## Can a Sea Anemone Walk Too?

Yes, it can. In the picture below you see that part of its foot is touching a rock. It slides that part along slowly and moves its body in that way. Sometimes it will lift its foot and put it on something else. Some sea anemones will even get on a shell that a hermit crab is using. As the crab moves it takes the sea anemone along.

It slides its foot along.

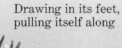

Drawing in its feet, pulling itself along

It can also lift its foot and put it on something else.

And sometimes it hitches a ride.

Why Does a Sea Anemone Keep Opening and Closing?

ANSWER The sea anemone has tentacles that look like flower petals. It uses the tentacles to catch food. The sea anemone pulls the food into its mouth with its tentacles and closes itself up. Then it opens again. The sea anemone also closes itself up when low tide leaves it out of water or when an enemy attacks.

Come over here!

I'm getting a free ride.

▲ **Green sea anemone**
Now it's open.

▲ **The same animal**
Now it's closed.

It closes up when
it's not in water.

If you touch it
it closes up.

Danger! Close up!

Is This a Fish?

ANSWER No, it's a jellyfish. Unlike a fish, it has no bones and few muscles. Most of its body is made of water. A jellyfish floats on the water, going wherever the current takes it.

▲ It grows and grows until it becomes an adult.

How Are Jellyfish Born?

They come from eggs. When jellyfish first hatch, they fasten themselves to a rock or some other object in the water. They slowly grow into the shape of a shallow bowl. Then they start looking like a flower with its petals stuck together. The petals drop off, one by one, and begin swimming around. Each petal is really a baby jellyfish.

▲ Jellyfish eggs.

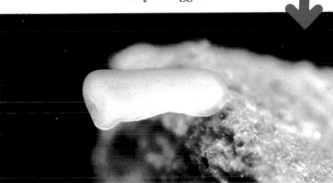

▲ It fastens itself to a rock.

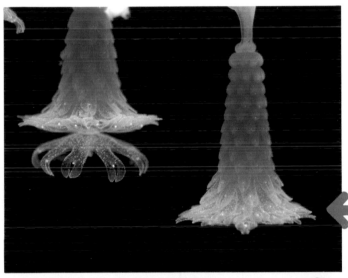

▲ Each petal will turn into a jellyfish.

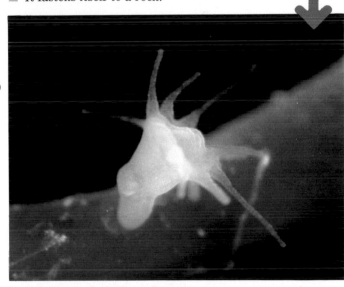

▲ It begins to look like a flower.

▲ The petals separate and become jellyfish.

● **To the Parent**

There are many kinds of jellyfish, most of which are shaped like an umbrella or bell. The top is made of a thick layer of a gelatinous material. Because its body is 99% water and has no bones or muscles, the jellyfish is hardly able to move under its own power. Instead it floats in the water. One stage of the jellyfish's life cycle is in the form of a stationary polyp, followed by that of a free-floating adult.

❓ Did You Know That a Starfish Can Replace a Lost Arm?

(ANSWER) If a starfish's arm breaks off, a new one will grow back. Even if a starfish is cut in half, two new starfish will result. As long as a portion of the body, or disc, is still attached to an arm, a new starfish will be generated. Some starfish can form new bodies just by breaking off parts of themselves.

A starfish breaks off its arm to escape from an attacking conch.

Its arm (lower left) is almost totally restored.

With only one arm it grows back to its old shape.

Some Other Animals That Can Grow Back Broken Parts

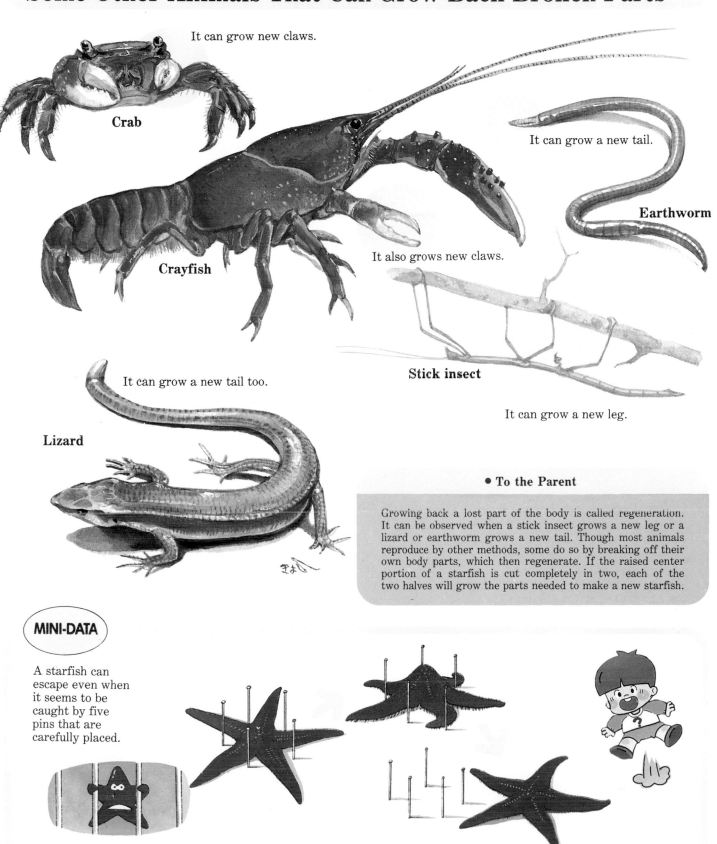

It can grow new claws.

Crab

It can grow a new tail.

Earthworm

Crayfish

It also grows new claws.

Stick insect

It can grow a new leg.

It can grow a new tail too.

Lizard

● **To the Parent**

Growing back a lost part of the body is called regeneration. It can be observed when a stick insect grows a new leg or a lizard or earthworm grows a new tail. Though most animals reproduce by other methods, some do so by breaking off their own body parts, which then regenerate. If the raised center portion of a starfish is cut completely in two, each of the two halves will grow the parts needed to make a new starfish.

MINI-DATA

A starfish can escape even when it seems to be caught by five pins that are carefully placed.

Do Mermaids Really Exist?

ANSWER People have told stories about mermaids for a long time. But there aren't really any mermaids. Maybe the stories got started when people saw a dugong or some other sea animal holding its young the way a woman might do with a child.

People Once Thought These Were Mermaids

▲ **Manatee.** It lives in tropical waters on both sides of the Atlantic Ocean. The manatee is the one with the round tail.

▲ **Dugong.** The split-tailed dugong lives in the Pacific and Indian Oceans. This one has sucker sharks on its side.

▲ **Ringed seal.** It lives in the cold waters of the Arctic. It eats many sea animals including fish, crabs and shellfish.

▲ **Fur seal.** Males winter near Alaska. Females and pups go to California. They mate in summer in the Bering Sea.

Hmmm! Some mermaids!

● **To the Parent**

In Chinese and Japanese the term for mermaid means "human fish." In the Western world, mermaids were thought to have the head, arms and body of a beautiful woman and the tail of a fish. Belief in the existence of these mythical creatures may have been inspired by sailors' sightings of dugongs or manatees. From a distance those sea mammals can look almost like humans as they hold themselves upright in the water and sometimes appear to be cuddling or suckling their offspring.

❓ Do Sea Plants Have Roots?

ANSWER No. Sea plants do not need them. Plants that live on land need roots to take in water and food. But sea plants get everything they need from the water all around them. Sea plants do have growths at the bottom that look like roots. They use them to hold onto rocks and other things in the water. That keeps plants from being carried away by the sea's currents.

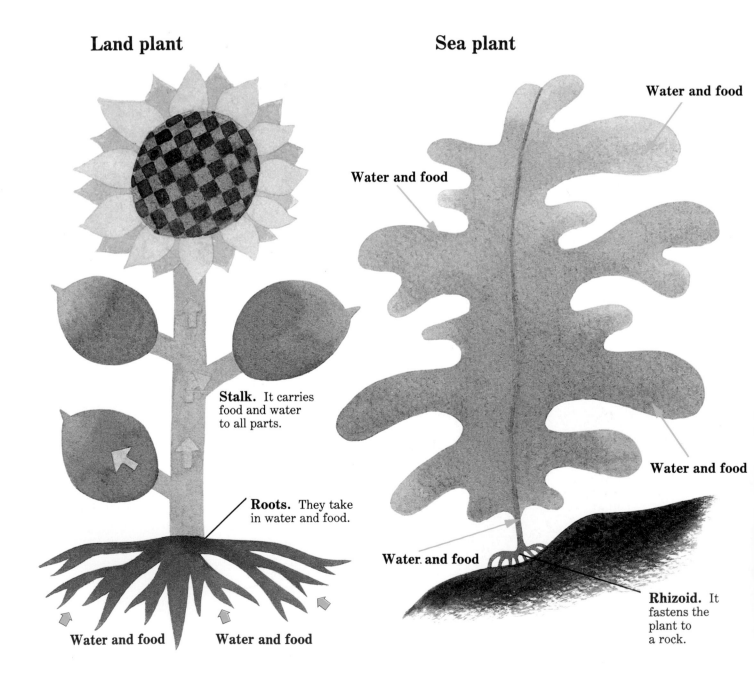

Land plant

Sea plant

Stalk. It carries food and water to all parts.

Roots. They take in water and food.

Water and food

Water and food

Water and food

Water and food

Water and food

Water and food

Water. and food

Rhizoid. It fastens the plant to a rock.

Do Sea Plants Have Flowers?

Land plants have flowers, and the flowers make seeds. New plants grow from the seeds. But sea plants have no flowers. Instead, they have small lumps called spores. New sea plants grow from the spores.

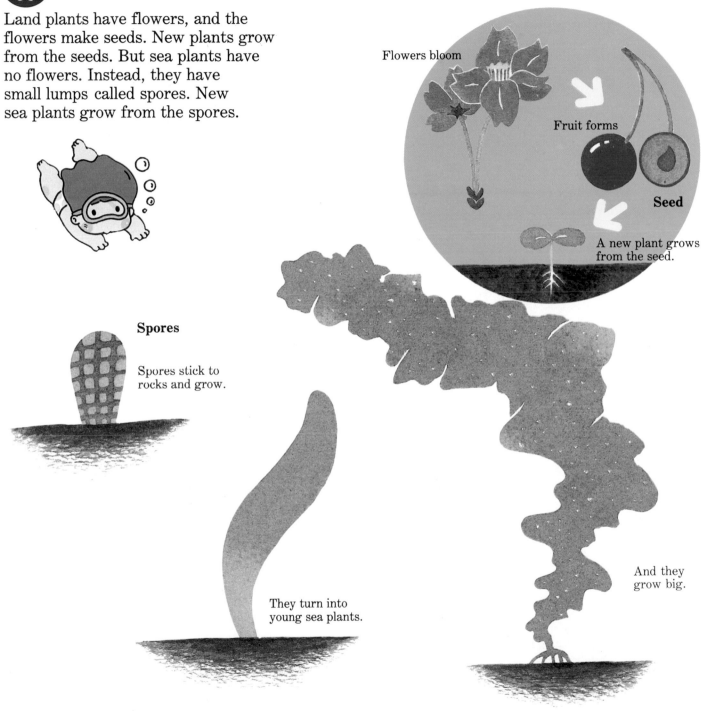

Flowers bloom

Fruit forms

Seed

A new plant grows from the seed.

Spores

Spores stick to rocks and grow.

They turn into young sea plants.

And they grow big.

● **To the Parent**

The parts of a sea plant are almost the same in structure, with no distinct roots, stems or leaves. What looks like a root is actually a rhizoid. The roots of a land plant absorb water and nutrients, but the rhizoid is nothing more than an anchor. A sea plant is described as foliate, or leaf-shaped, because the whole plant appears to be merely a single leaf.

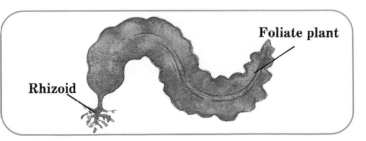

Foliate plant

Rhizoid

? How Do Tadpoles Turn into Frogs?

ANSWER Frogs lay eggs, and tadpoles hatch from these eggs. The tadpoles grow back legs first and then front ones. Their tails get shorter. Finally they come up onto the land as frogs.

SPRING

A clump of eggs

The eggs hatch into tadpoles. At first they can't swim very well, so they hang onto things around them.

■ Kinds of tadpoles

▲ **Tadpole of a toad**

▲ **Tadpole of a leopard frog**

▲ **Tadpole of a bullfrog**

FALL

Finally it can come up onto land.

SUMMER

■ **Life of a leopard frog**

The tail gets shorter.

The front legs grow.

The tadpole grows larger and learns to swim well.

It grows back legs.

▲ **Tadpole of a tree frog**

▲ **Tadpole of a green forest frog**

● **To the Parent**

A frog lays eggs, but its young first go through a tadpole stage, a change in form that is called metamorphosis. A tadpole uses gills to get oxygen. When the tadpole first hatches, its gills are exposed, but they gradually recede beneath the skin as the tadpole grows. Even a full-grown frog lacks lungs. It breathes through its skin, which must be kept moist. Thus it is at home both on land and in the water.

What Do Frogs Do in Winter?

ANSWER During the cold winter, a frog sleeps underground. In other words, it hibernates. Before it hibernates, the frog eats just as much as it can. In this way the frog stores up enough food to last through its long winter sleep.

▲ **A hibernating frog**

Before a frog hibernates it eats lots of food.

When leaves fall it feels chilly.

It sleeps until spring comes.

When it gets cold the frog digs in.

Do Other Animals Hibernate?

Snakes, turtles, bears and other animals hibernate too.

▲ **Snake.** It hibernates in the ground.

▲ **Turtle.** It hibernates in the mud.

▲ **Dormouse.** It is curled up in a hole in a tree, where it's hibernating.

▲ **Bats.** They wrap themselves up with their wings and hibernate in caves.

● **To the Parent**

In cold-blooded animals like frogs, snakes and turtles the body temperature conforms to that of the surroundings and will drop drastically with the coming of cold weather. The animal stops moving entirely as it goes into hibernation. Warm-blooded animals like bears, however, do not experience such a great drop in body temperature. Their winter-season hibernation is more like an extended period of half-sleep.

Why Don't Tree Frogs Fall?

(ANSWER) On the ends of a tree frog's toes are pads that work like suckers. With those toe pads the frog can hold on tightly to trees or grass. It won't fall even if it hangs upside down. Because the tree frog's toes are long and will bend easily, it can hang onto the branches as it walks.

▲ Toe pads gripping glass

▼ Tree frog on a bamboo stalk

A Tree Frog's Body

■ Its body is always wet

A tree frog breathes through its skin. It gives off a slimy fluid to keep its skin wet all the time.

If its skin dries out it will die.

Hiding on a tree.

■ Its body changes color

A tree frog's body changes color to match what's around it so that enemies can't see it. On a tree branch it's brown, but in the grass it turns green.

■ It croaks when rain is coming

Before a rain the air gets moist. A frog can tell when there is more moisture in the air, and it croaks. This is a sign that rain is coming.

■ Its tongue catches insects

In an instant, a frog can stick out its tongue and catch an insect. It will not eat insects that are not moving. But it will eat anything near it that moves.

● To the Parent

Tree frogs are very sensitive to the amount of moisture in air. When it increases with the approach of rain, they croak noisily as if they are happy. This amphibian is about 1.5 inches (4 cm) long. It has adhesive toe pads to help it hold onto grass and tree branches, and it can even hang upside down with them. These frogs feed primarily on insects and spiders.

? Why Do Frogs Croak?

ANSWER Only males croak; females do not. The male has a special sac in his throat, called a vocal sac. He puffs the sac full of air and makes a croaking sound. Croaking is the way he attracts a female mate.

Leopard frog croaking

Toad laying its eggs

A tree frog

▲ A green tree frog croaking

An Asian green tree frog laying eggs in foam

▲ **Tree Frog.** It croaks by puffing up the vocal sac under its chin.

◀ A toad croaking

● **To the Parent**

Frogs croak during their mating season. The male frogs sit by ponds and streams and call other frogs by croaking. The assembled frogs form into pairs, then go off to mate and lay their eggs. The little tree frog also croaks during wet spells when it senses a drop in atmospheric pressure. Its croaking tells us that the weather will soon take a turn for the worse.

? Did You Know That Turtles Can Catch Fish?

(ANSWER) Of course turtles can catch fish. Most people think a turtle can't move fast at all, but sometimes it does. It will move up on a fish very quietly in the dark when the fish is sleeping. Then quick as a flash it will catch the fish in its mouth and eat it.

▼ **A turtle catching a fish**

A Turtle's Life

It sleeps during the day and is active at night.

A turtle suns itself out of the water — on a rock, for instance. It does this so it won't get mold or insects on its shell.

Turtles can swim through the water very quietly.

Turtles like to eat fish, shrimp, crayfish and the like. But they will also eat water plants.

TRY THIS

You can keep turtles in an aquarium. They need a large stone so they can sun themselves. But be careful how you place the stone. You don't want the turtle to use it as a stepping stone to escape!

A turtle's food

Fish   Shrimp   Apples   Carrots

How Do Turtles Fit Inside Their Shells?

ANSWER Turtles have soft bones. They bend very easily. When a turtle pulls its head, legs and tail inside its shell, it carefully folds them. The pictures here show you how the turtle does it.

■ **Side view**

The bones are all folded inside.

■ **Bottom view**

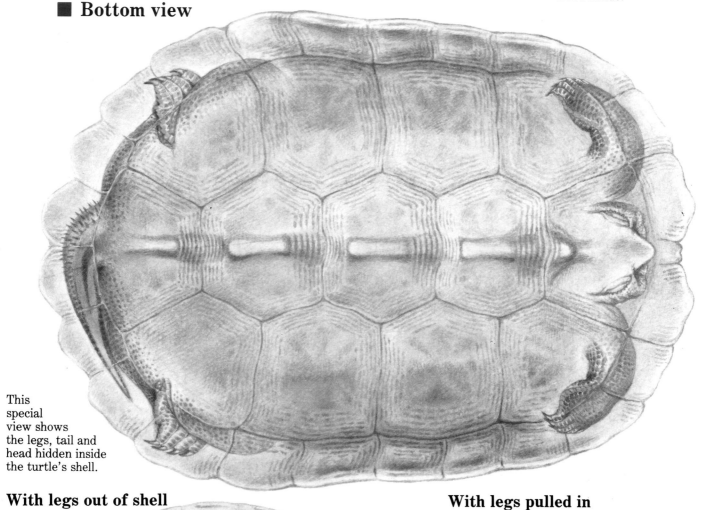

This special view shows the legs, tail and head hidden inside the turtle's shell.

With legs out of shell

With legs pulled in

76

But Why Do They Pull in Their Legs?

Turtles pull their head, legs and tail into their shell if they think they're in danger, or when they want to rest or sleep. They also do it when they're in hibernation during the winter.

When a turtle feels that danger is near, it pulls in its head, legs and tail for a while. That's the way the turtle protects itself.

▲ Looking into the face of a turtle. Does it scare you?

The turtle sleeps with its head, legs and tail tucked safely into its shell.

When winter comes a turtle hibernates in mud at the bottom of a pond or river.

● **To the Parent**

A turtle's shell is fused to the backbone, and the ribs are flattened and widened for more support. Turtles have no way to defend themselves other than by withdrawing their exposed head, legs and tail back into their shell. The neck, which is flexible, is retracted in an S curve to perform this maneuver.

❓ What Have We Here?

■ Sea hare's eggs

The sea hare's eggs are long and thin. They look a lot like noodles.

■ One sea urchin's spines

Some of this sea urchin's spines are short, and some are shaped like a trumpet.

■ A shellfish's eggs

This shellfish mixes its eggs with sand, then forms them into the shape of a bowl.

■ Octopus eggs

The eggs are laid in holes in rocks. Below are the young.

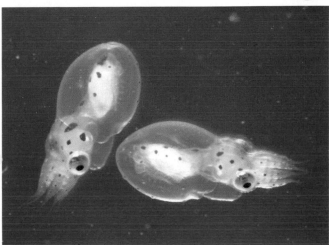

■ A young salamander

The feathery things on the head are its gills.

■ A crab's sand balls

One type of crab eats small grubs and insects that live in the sand. As it eats them it takes in sand too. The crab makes sand balls like these out of the sand.

● To the Parent

The pictures of the sea hare, shellfish and octopus seen here illustrate the variety of eggs found in the animal kingdom. Salamanders are amphibians and like frogs develop in a larval stage in water. Their gills disappear as their lungs develop. Though crabs are sea creatures, many like the one you see here may spend large portions of their lives on land.

❓ And What Do We Have Here?

■ Salmon hatching from their eggs

Salmon eggs hatch as winter ends and spring begins. The small young fish are called fry. The fry stay for a while in the rivers where they were born. Then, about the end of spring, they swim downstream and out into the ocean.

■ The rectal opening of a sea urchin

This is where a sea urchin lets out waste. The mouth is on the other side.

● To the Parent

When salmon eggs have been fertilized they absorb water and become more resilient, so that they are not easily crushed. Salmon fry are nourished at first by the yolk, which remains with their body. When this source of nourishment is used up, they begin hunting for prey. The sea urchin shown here is but one of many species. Its poisonous spines break off easily.

Growing-Up Album

Water Animals

Some of the water animals shown on these pages live in the oceans, while others live in fresh water. Can you figure out which ones live where?

Octopus

Turtle

Globefish

Starfish

Catfish

Salt water

In the oceans: Octopus, globefish, starfish, sea urchin, scallop, flying fish and shark. Some catfish live in salt water, and some live in fresh water. The same thing is true of turtles.

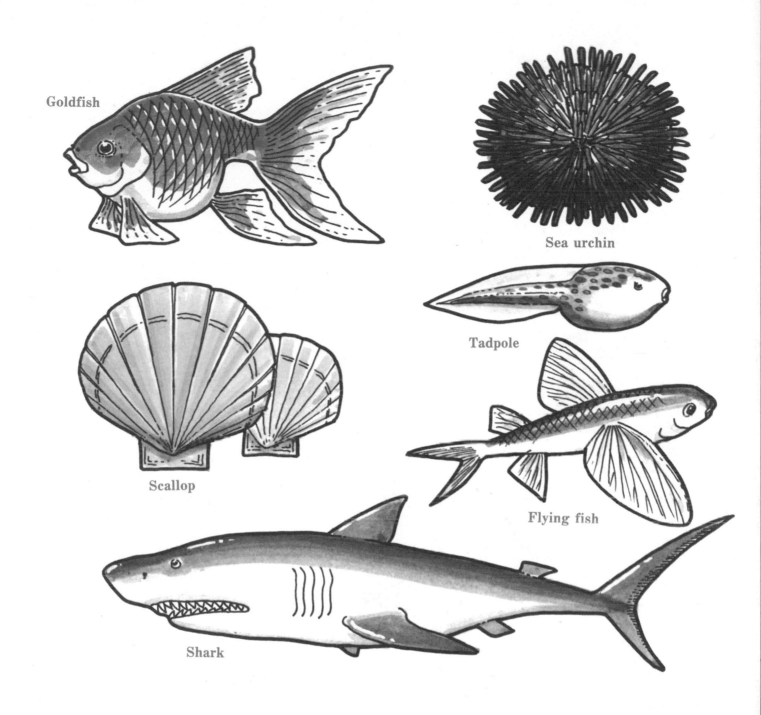

Goldfish

Sea urchin

Scallop

Tadpole

Flying fish

Shark

Fresh water

In rivers, lakes and ponds: Goldfish, tadpole, turtle and catfish. The catfish and turtle shown here are fresh-water ones, but there are other turtles and catfish that live in salt water.

Sink or Float?

Now that your child is curious about life in the water, she may be interested in water too. This game can help her learn more. Collect some of the common items shown on this page. Fill a large glass bowl with water. Have your child hold each item and guess whether it will sink or float. Then have her put it in the water and see what happens. Finally have her draw each item where she thinks it belongs in the tank on the next page. Have her try other household items that she might think of.

Apple

Crayon

Pencil

Spoon

Brush

Key

Egg

Paper clips

Stone

Stick

Aluminium foil

These will float: _____

These will sink:_____

Who's Catching What?

All the animals are fishing in a pond. Follow the fishing line to find out who has caught what. Who has caught the old rubber boot? And who's going to get the big carp?

A Child's First Library of Learning

Life in the Water

Time-Life Books Inc.
is a wholly owned subsidiary of
Time Incorporated
Time-Life Books, Alexandria, Virginia
Children's Publishing

Director: Robert H. Smith
Associate Director: E. A. Wotkyns III
Editorial Director: Neil Kagan
Promotional Director: Kathy Tresnak
Editorial Consultants: Jacqueline A. Ball
Andrew Gutelle

Editorial Supervision by:

**International Editorial Services Inc.
Tokyo, Japan**

Editor: C. E. Berry
Writer: Winston S. Priest
Translation: Ronald K. Jones
Editorial Assistants: Keiko Minagawa
Alison Hashimoto
Misao Sawa
Miki Ishii
Design: Kim Bolitho
Educational Consultants: Laurie Hanawa
Janette Bryden

**TIME
LIFE** ®

Library of Congress Cataloging in Publication Data
Life in the water
p. cm.—(A Child's first library of learning)
Summary: Questions and answers present information about
aquatic animals such as sharks, crabs, fish, frogs, and barnacles.
Includes an activities section.
ISBN 0-8094-4853-X   ISBN 0-8094-4854-8 (lib. bdg.)
1. Aquatic fauna—Miscellanea—Juvenile literature. [1. Aquatic
animals—Miscellanea. 2. Questions and answers.] I. Time-Life
Books. II. Series.
QL120.L54 1989   591.92—dc19   88-36633   CIP   AC

©1989 Time-Life Books Inc.
©1983 Gakken Co. Ltd.
Fourth printing 1992. Printed in U.S.A.
Published simultaneously in Canada.

TIME-LIFE is a trademark of Time Incorporated U.S.A.

Time-Life Books Inc. offers a wide range of fine publications,
including home video products. For subscription information, call
1-800-621-7026 or write TIME-LIFE BOOKS, P.O. Box C-32068,
Richmond, Virginia 23261-2068.